7 SECRETS OF TRANSFORMATION

7 Secrets of Transformation

A PATH TO LIMITLESS DREAMS

Swapnil Bharate

BLISS Books

Contents

Dedication

This book is dedicated to my late mother Lata Ashok Bharate for igniting the physical fitness spark in me at an early age and passing the baton of her leadership skills, and to my late brother-in-law Hrishikesh Gijare for imbibing the conscientiousness and hardworking qualities in me during my youth. I am eternally grateful to both of you.

Acknowledgements

The first bow of gratitude to the Supreme for guiding me through this life journey, for nourishing the thought, and directing me to generate this piece of work. My belief in the divine presence is the source of my strength and inspiration in all the good deeds. The spiritual foundation laid by Shri Samartha Ramdas Swami provides me clarity and purpose to navigate through life challenges and serve the wider community.

I am profoundly grateful to my grandparents, my father Ashok Bharate, late mother Lata Bharate for their unconditional love and being my constant pillars of strength and wisdom to shape me into what I am today. Equally, my siblings Manisha, Manjusha, and Amit have been by my side throughout, always encouraging, guiding, and nurturing an environment influencing my growth and character.

My better half Pallavi and our two daughters, Shriya and Shravya are my source of energy, my supporting rocks in thick and thin and my motivators and critiques helping me to grow and succeed in all my pursuits. Without their profound love and affection, none of my achievements would be possible. Thanks, my darlings.

Friends have always been an important part of my life. Their companionship has been a source of joy and encouragement. Their presence, invaluable advice and comfort through my highs and lows are appreciated with thanks.

Mentors and Coaches have a major role in my personal growth. Since childhood, various saints and their scriptures have helped me learn and grow my philosophical and spiritual base.

With age and time mentors and coaches like Shri Samartha Ramdas Swami, APJ Abdul Kalam, Swami Vivekananda, Tony Robbins, Simon Sinek, Robin Sharma, John C Maxwell, Jim Rohn, Stephen R Covey, Rhonda Byrne, and many others have been instrumental in my personal and professional growth through their Books, Seminars and Podcasts. Their insights, guidance, motivation, and inspiration are continuously molding me into a better version of myself.

Last but not least, my thanks to Hem Singh Patle and Manoj Sonawane for encouraging me to initiate this book project, rekindling my long-term goal, and guiding me throughout this process.

These acknowledgements cannot be enough without a special mention to all my social media followers and friends whom I treasure dearly. You are my constant source of energy and support towards building a happy and healthy community.

Love and Gratitude!
Swapnil Bharate

Foreword

Our mind processes more than 60,000 thoughts in a day. Book writing is like giving a pause to your fast-paced life and noting down some of the thoughts from this huge number.

As we grow old, we tell our life story to the new generation of our family. We share with them both the struggle, and success part of our life and which has the power to change their life as well. As Patrick Rothfuss said in this quote *"It's like everyone tells a story about themselves inside their own head. Always. All the time. That story makes you what you are. We build ourselves out of that story."* When we write a book, we go one step ahead and bring out that content from our head to paper and share it, not only with our family members but also with the whole world.

This book highlights to the readers these 7 dimensions of life: spiritual, physical, intellectual, professional, financial, family, and social as well as tools, techniques, and concepts which have the power to transform our existence.

Swapnil has done an excellent work by bringing out his life's lessons and all the important aspects of his life in this book.

Pause for a while, and read something new and take your life to the next level.

Learning and adding value to people's lives is key to our life's success. Always find the opportunity to be in these two zones.

Happy Reading

Manoj Sonawane

1

My Journey

I was born into a middle-class family in Pune, India. I am the third of four siblings. Pune, renowned as India's educational and cultural epicenter, provided a rich background to my upbringing, a fact that fills me with immense pride. My father dedicated his career to semi-government service, while my mother, a commerce graduate, prioritized our family over her professional aspirations. However, through tutoring, she contributed financially, aiding in the management of the household alongside my dad. My mother cultivated the leadership quality in me. She was instrumental in shaping my character and values. I am very attached to my mother. My father was the driving force behind my academic pursuits, steering me towards engineering—a field I embraced due to his influence and guidance. Without a clear direction in my early years, it was his vision that illuminated the path ahead.

Over the course of 13 years in India, I worked for two companies and was enriched by the personal milestones of marriage and the birth of two daughters. Although my life had many ups and downs at that time, but I had my parents, family, and friends to support me. One of my cousins Mahesh Bhagwat who now happens to be the Additional DGP of Telangana State Police is and has been a mentor to me since my youth. All these people are like pillars of my foundation and were crucial to my upbringing. Even though my career was flourishing in those days, I felt I was missing something from the inside. The thought that I can do more than this has always been there on my mind. That's when I took my next step and applied for an international opportunity that led to a bigger life path.

2

Two Wheels of Life

Before I go into my life story further, let me share the background of my better half Pallavi. If I consider two wheels that run my life, then one wheel is my wife and another is me. Without her, the journey of my life would come to a standstill. She was born in Sangamner, a small town in the Ahmednagar district of India. Her educational journey began in the very school where her parents served as teachers, completing her secondary education there. Her academic pursuits then led her to Pune, where she attended Fergusson College for her higher secondary education, and then completed her Master's degree in Organic Chemistry from Pune University.

I married her in the year 2000. We resided in Pune, India, until our relocation to the United Kingdom in 2008. Between 2000 and 2008, she worked as a Lecturer at MIT Pharmacy College, D Y Patil College, Fergusson College, and Sangamner Science College.

Despite a successful career in India, Pallavi decided to start a new chapter with me in the UK, which meant she had to leave her established career. Upon our arrival in the UK, Pallavi experienced a period of adjustment, taking a year and a half to explore her professional options. She eventually found great success by starting her work as a science technician in some schools. For the last 8 years, she has been working as a Science teacher in a prestigious state secondary Grammar School.

The year 2017 marked a significant transition in our lives, with Pallavi initiating private tutoring alongside her teaching career and that was the great decision taken by her. When I was out of a job during the pandemic, she took the baton of the main breadwinner and supported me to sail through this challenging period. Today, her work has grown exponentially. As it is said, once a teacher is always a teacher. She is a very good teacher and word of mouth has spread her reputation.

Over the past three years, we have introduced group tuition sessions, further enhancing her educational impact. Today, she has regained her productive and flourishing career. She is an extremely hard-working lady who manages Grammar School work, tuition, and family all together. She has achieved success in reaching her goals with her utmost determination in everything she does.

She is a strong supporter in any of my work ventures including the decision to move to the UK, a choice that required starting anew. It was not easy to start from scratch and regain her life's work. It was a struggle for her in those initial years of her life in the UK, but her determination paid off and she claimed her career back. These ups and downs in life further strengthened our bond as a couple. We helped each other to pursue our dreams and decisions whether it's moving to a new country or starting Pallavi's career afresh.

3

Change Begins

****
"If an egg is broken by an outside force, life ends. If broken by an inside force, life begins. Great things always begin from the inside."

- Jim Kwik

I could say that change began in my life in the year 2017. I had all the expertise in the job I was doing at that time for my company. I was leading offshore and onshore responsibilities and had a good amount of experience in my work. In that period, the oil and gas industry was not doing well, so my company began laying off employees.

I was under the impression that my skills were indispensable to my employer, which gave me a sense of security. However, in October of that year, my confidence was shattered when my name appeared on the layoff list. It was an unprecedented low in my life. The thought started churning in my mind like "How can they do this?". I was serving and was so much loyal to them. This was also the moment for me to sit down and think about why this happened to me.

In our culture, we believe that there must be a reason for the thing that happens in our life. I discussed this with my wife and obviously, the first thing was to find a new job for me even though the overall market was not good. However, I eventually redirected my career path towards freelancing and consultancy, founding my company SP&SS Ltd. After two months of patience and trying to get a contract, I was offered one opportunity, and then I secured several other opportunities from various companies over the next 18 months.

Unfortunately, my success was short-lived. The decline of the oil and gas sector, compounded by the global pandemic, severely impacted my business. Facing this new challenge without a steady income and witnessing my venture struggle was profoundly distressing. During this period, I was engulfed in negativity and despair and reached the lowest point in my life.

We humans feel the worst of everything at such a level in our lives. I stopped all this noise in my mind and said to myself "Look, you have a family and they will suffer even though you are not there or not being active" and that's where my new beginning started. I got immense help from friends and family. It was my wife who was my backbone throughout all of this time. I hired professional coaches to help me come out of this situation. This was a journey which was up, down, and then up again.

Today, I find myself significantly better equipped than

I was in the past. Recently I had a conversation with my father-in-law in which he imparted some wisdom to me. He told me, "Swapnil, experiencing difficult times is crucial. It not only helps you appreciate the good days but also prepares you for any challenges that may lie ahead because that's the essence of being human."

4

Learning and Teaching

"Take the first step in faith. You don't have to see the whole staircase, just take the first step."
- Martin Luther King

Understanding oneself is the cornerstone of all wisdom. This principle is deeply embedded in our Indian culture, marked by its rich spiritual tradition. Among the texts that have significantly influenced my personal growth is "*Dasbodh*" by *Shri Samartha Ramdas Swami*. One of his teachings, "You will certainly reach your goal, but only if you start working towards it," has been particularly impactful. It also means you can't sit idle and do nothing and wait for things to happen. You have to take action. Take an example of mine, I would have taken actions in many ways like blaming others, and sulking when I was jobless. However, such approaches would not have been constructive. Instead, the path to overcoming life's challenges lies in taking lifeward actions. Also, I could sustain this life situation due to my spiritual background.

I had to let go of my old limitations and try something new. I once dreamed of working on subjects like Endurance and Excellence. It was the perfect time for me to use spiritual teachings to overcome life's challenges and set my own example which I did. Recognizing a widespread need for such guidance, I embarked on a journey to impart my wisdom through tutoring, mentoring, training, and coaching. This compilation of experiences and insights eventually evolved into the publication of my book, "7 Secrets of Transformation: A Path to Limitless Dreams." This work delves into the seven pivotal dimensions of life: spiritual, physical, intellectual, professional, financial, familial, and social, advocating for a comprehensive approach to mastering life's challenges.

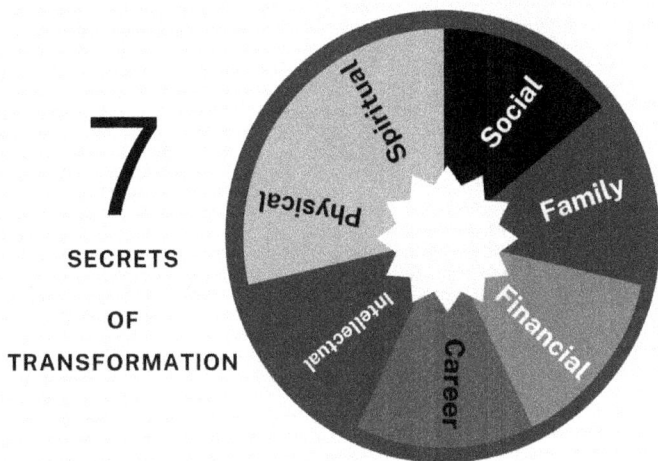

Figure 1: Seven Secrets of Transformations

A person needs holistic knowledge to overcome any life challenges. Let's learn about the first element of this dimension that is spirituality in the next chapter.

5

Secret 1: The Power of Spirituality

****

"Aham Brahmasmi (I am the Universe), Tat Tvam Asi (You are that)."

- Upanishad

The realization of the existence of the supreme power was introduced to me by my grandmother and I am indebted to her for this knowledge. As a child, she used to take me to the temple wherein the teachings laid the foundation of my philosophical and spiritual journey. All her knowledge helped me to build my connections with God. I realized my purpose of living. We are not here just to satisfy our senses. As a human, we have to develop our soul and that needs profound spiritual knowledge. I am fortunate that I started this journey at an early age of my life.

We use the five senses (skin, ears, eyes, nose, and tongue) to feel this 3-dimensional (3D) world and believe only in things or matter that we perceive with these senses but you need to go beyond that (five senses) if you want to advance in your spiritual journey.

You can make connections with God if you leave this sensory world and enter a meditative state and become nothing.

Let's learn how here:

Ask the monk and he will answer you that we are just a spark of the divine and part of this one consciousness. It's a world of potential and all dimensions exist here, all past, present, and future events exist here. You can create anything by using the power of this consciousness. That's God. But understand here, you have to become nothing to create everything. Leave your old baggage behind and that helps you to order from the menu of universal consciousness. You can do this by being in the present moment and creating life seeds (thoughts) that grow into great trees and give you fruits (achievements).

Secondly, the things you do bad for others is doing to yourself only because at that level you are part of that one consciousness and that's the reason the person who cheats on others gets cheated by many others. You can't escape from the eye of consciousness. It's observing all of us for every moment.

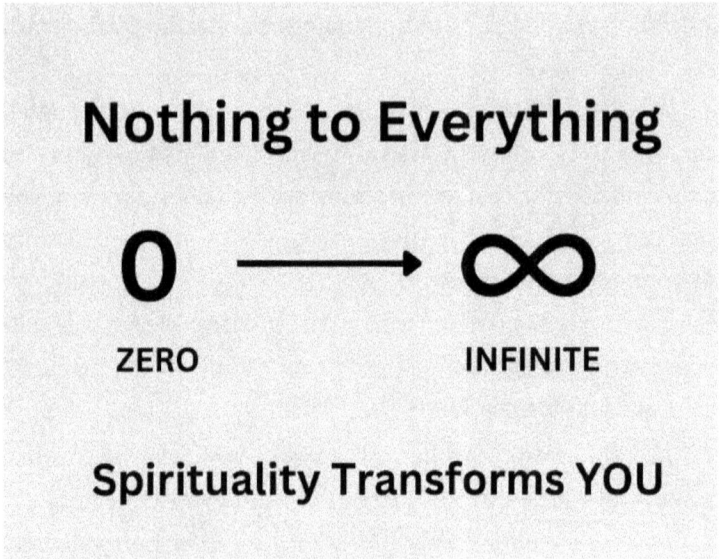

Nothing to Everything

0 → **∞**

ZERO   **INFINITE**

Spirituality Transforms YOU

Figure 2: Seven Secrets of Transformations

Now let's explore the health aspect in the next chapter.

Actions Points:

1. Which family member planted the seed of spirituality in you?

2. Have you experienced divine help or guidance in your life? What form did you receive it in?

6

Secret 2: The Health: A Basis for All Achievements

"Take care of your body. It's the only place you have to live."

- Jim Rohn

It happened that my dad was posted in Nashik, India and that is also the hometown of my mother. It was the happiest childhood I ever had. At that time, I was surrounded by loads of uncles. It became a ritual for us to go on outings every weekend. We visited all the places of Nashik, including temples. These moments of my life lasted for just a limited period and I faced the first health challenge in my life when I was in Grade 3. I developed a skin condition called Psoriasis at an early age. Initially, we did not know what this skin condition is. My parents visited various doctors. We tried everything including Allopathy, Ayurveda, etc. but could not figure out what to do? Or how to deal with it? We were jumping from one treatment to another. It never subsided and was growing at a faster pace. It was a traumatic experience for me. I had to always wear a full-sleeved shirt and long trousers to hide it. People started questioning me about this skin condition and I was too young to answer them. I also started to develop an inferiority complex and felt that I was not as good as other kids. I was unable to participate in all the outdoor activities or games. Even though I was participating, I was holding myself three to four steps back while playing. It was the most traumatic experience of my childhood. As a result, my parents were taking utmost care of me, and they tried every possible treatment, whether they were recommended by a known or unknown person. When we moved to Pune my skin condition aggravated as the climate here is drier and cold. This skin condition had covered my face. It had flaky and dry skin. When I peeled it up the part of that skin was getting red. I had to continuously moisturize it with cream. Psoriasis is a non-contagious skin condition but at that time it made my life horrible as people were staring at me, asking me various questions. My school at Pune allowed me to wear a full-sleeve shirt (between 4th standard to 10th standard) to avoid all this. I always felt bad about it, specifically when we were growing up and seeing everyone on the playground during physical education classes and cricket. I was exceptional among all of them as I had to wear the school uniform that was covering my whole body to avoid all questioning.

All of the other students were wearing their PE clothes and playing freely. It was hurting me a lot. Sometimes my soul screamed and said "God why me"? It had a negative impact on my mental health during my growing-up years.

I had avoided all other health activities like gym and swimming. It took me many years to start all this. I started swimming when I was in the degree college. It also made me realize that it's a life and anything can happen to us. This skin condition kept me away from all extracurricular or sporty activities.

As an adult when I look back now, I realize it is a common skin condition that grows abnormally at some parts of the body and mostly in patches (and it erupts seasonally- it aggravates in the cold season and subsides during summer). It's just an extra layer of skin as compared to the normal skin. It needs three to four times moisturization to keep it healthy. Even though I live in London and the environment here is very much cold as compared to Pune, but I am making sure to keep not only my skin healthy but also my whole body. Friends and family know that over the years I have evolved from a physically shy and body-conscious person to a fit and confident individual, hard to guess that I am in the fifties club.

I transformed myself tremendously. I have conquered both the physical and mental realms of my body through my Bodybuilding Journey. It wasn't a cakewalk to venture into a sport like such almost in one's fifties. It demands an extreme level of willpower, consistency, and dedication. But with tremendous support from family, friends, and coaches, I was able to reach the British Finals (BNBF – Oct 2022). If life throws challenges at you, then turn them into opportunities. As a result of these events in my life, I realized I would always take care of my body.

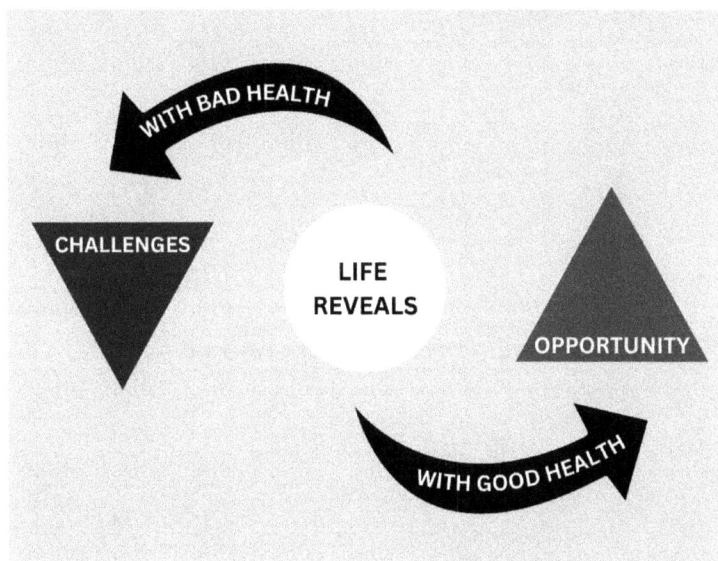

Figure 3: Life Revelations

We need to train both the mind and body to deal with most health challenges.

Let's learn the intellectual aspects of life in the next chapter.

Actions Points:

1. Name the health exercise you've been delaying. Explain how adding it to your workout could benefit you.

2. What help do you need to improve your health?

7

Secret 3: Intellectual: A Key Ingredient of Life

****

"If we encounter a man of rare intellect, we should ask him what books he reads."

- Ralph Waldo Emerson

You have a great career, you're increasing your income sources every year, you've achieved the target of your optimum health, you've improved relationships with your family members, and also had a great social life. But when you look back and analyze your knowledge needle, you find that you haven't sharpened it yet. You know that this needle is helpful because it works like a compass that always shows the required direction to you. The process of learning requires a lot of reading. The more you read (or gain knowledge) the more you sharpen it. It's that simple. Anyone who begins the personal transformation journey always starts it by reading a book, or anyone who feels stuck or stagnant in life, then they go and buys a bunch of books from the bookstores. We need ideas to grow in life and that comes from new learning. Books are the cheapest and fastest way to get ideas.

Your reading pipeline should never drain. You have to fill it up consistently. Ask yourself what's my next read? Your reading list should include subjects like philosophy, spirituality, science, and life or whatever interest you pick it up and read it. Solve the various curiosities of your life. Libraries are filled with biographies of people who left many clues for living a great life.

As mentioned in an earlier chapter, the first book that helped me to transform my life completely was the spiritual scriptures *Dasbodh* by *Shri Samartha Ramdas Swami.* Personal, professional, and family aspects of life are covered in this book. By using the insights from this book, you can deal with any life situation.

There must be at least one book that must have inspired you.

Here are some ways that may help you to read many books:

1. Consider a book as an idea and you decode it by reading it.
2. The right book can save millions of dollars if you buy

it at the right time. See what that next book will be for me.

3. Buying books and learning something new from them brings more excitement, and you build such momentum by reading books regularly. Let's call it the "joy of reading".

4. Discuss about the books in your social circle and they may inspire you to read many great books.

What is a temporary alternative for mentors?

If your circumstances limit you to hire a mentor, then books can serve as a temporary alternative for it. In fact, reading books before looking for mentors will fill the gap fast as compared to hiring a mentor directly. Let's learn how to use books as a temporary alternative for mentors below.

List out books and writers of your mentor traits and convert them into living teachers as much as possible. It has double advantages as it provides the knowledge to you written by past and present masters in your field. Through some imagination on your part, you turn them into a living presence. You ask yourself what would they do in this situation or that? In this way, you can attempt to find the answers to many of your questions. Eventually, books will solve many of your life's puzzles and also help you find your perfect mentor. As a result of knowing the perfect mentor traits through books, you will be able to recognize them when you meet him/her.

Example of a perfect mentor

Countless army generals have used Napoleon Bonaparte's

traits through books to solve their battlefield puzzles. Fill the gap of your mentor till the time you find him/her by reading books.

Build your reading list in such a way that fuels your growth. As said by Jim Rohn in one of his quotes: "Miss a meal if you have to, but don't miss a book". There must be a depth in it.

In the next chapter, we will learn how to turn a career into a mission.

Action Points:

1. Write the name of the book that helped you in your life. (It's an exercise to reconnect you with reading)

2. Build your reading list here.

8

Secret 4: Transform Your Career into Mission

****

"Vision sees the stars; mission carves the path to reach them."
- Aloo Denish Obiero

In this book, I have previously detailed my professional journey. Later, I made a significant transition in my life and shifted my focus from a career to a mission. This decision gave a significant push to my life. Embracing a career path impacts only a few hundred of lives, but pursuing a mission carries the power to impact the lives of millions.

All of us begin our life with some career. But there are very few who build their career around passion and then convert it into a mission. It's a truth that real success is not in a career but in a mission. If you have a choice, then choose a mission over a career.

Life becomes self-centered if you build it around a career. But if you build it around a mission, then it becomes people-oriented. Let me explain it by using my mission statement below.

"My mission is to transform over one million lives into successful lives in the next five years through my books, writing, and teaching".

The above statement defines my life path. I am obliged to work for it. It channelizes my time, energy, and resources towards it.

That's the reason I wrote this book, designed my training programs, and conducted seminars and webinars to impact the life of other people. I am also using various social media platforms and sharing my life learning that helps me to reach more people.

My ultimate goal is to impact lives through my mission.

Most of the masters in the past have followed this path and left their footprint in the world by serving people and they use the mission to accomplish their goal.

If you want to impact people's lives through life's work, then create your mission. That's the way to achieve massive success in life.

In the next chapter, let's examine the meaningful aspects of money in our life.

Action Points:

1. Write your mission statement below:

2. Write down different ways to serve people in your mission:

9

Secret 5: How to Use Money in Creating a Meaningful Life

****

"It's not how much money you make, but how much money you keep, how hard it works for you, and how many generations you keep it for."

- Robert Kiyosaki

Money, undeniably, plays a vital role and shapes our life journey. However, a significant gap remains in our education about the true aspects of money. It's a subject that is often overlooked by both parents and educational institutions. In reality, money is more than a financial instrument. If I had known about these true aspects of money earlier in life, I would not have been in debt.

The following is a list of these aspects of money:

1. Money has a purpose
2. Money has emotions
3. Money is spiritual

It wasn't until later in my career that I learned about these three aspects of money, which holds greater significance than the investment elements. Let's learn about it here in details.

1. Money Has a Purpose

Earning money for riches and earning money for purpose are two different things; therefore, according to above statement we can categorize money into two categories:

A) Purposeless money

B) Purposeful money

The first one (A) is short-lived because money lacks a purpose here while the latter one (B) is long-lasting as it gives a purpose to your money and defines the path along for more success.

A person in the first situation (A) builds a castle on the sand while the latter one (B) builds the whole empire on a solid foundation and protects each of its houses.

A person in the first situation indicates a poor mindset. Money operates primarily as a psychological construct, and devoid of a specific purpose, it loses its emotional significance. Anchor your financial goals to a clear purpose for enduring prosperity. Now let's discuss the emotion part of money.

2) Money has Emotion

*"Your emotions are the slaves to your thoughts, and you are the slave to your emotions." -**Elizabeth Gilbert***

The amount of money you earn is always proportionate to your purpose. The bigger the purpose, the bigger the money. But if you bind the purpose with emotion, then it becomes a powerful combination and it helps you achieve any goal, including earning money. Let's take the example of a marriage proposal here (to explain it). If a prospective bride rejects the proposal from the groom on the grounds of his poverty, and if this person binds the **emotion of rejection** as a reason to get rich (purpose), then chances are high that he can become rich.

Let's take another example, that is the **emotion of hunger and poverty**. A person on the verge to die due to hunger and poverty and if she somehow survives and had the realization that she would never see or live days like these. Then a person of such the lowest level of life is more likely to become rich because she binds the emotion (hunger and poverty) with a purpose (becoming rich). She will do whatever it takes to get out of that situation. Thus, emotion with purpose makes you an extraordinary person. If you have a purpose, then add emotion to it. It will take you to places beyond your imagination.

We all have life incidences where we need money. Tap the most potential incident and bind emotion to it and that's enough to get to the root of money. You will find many ways to get rich and create wealth for you.

3) Money is Spiritual

Money is spiritual and that's the reason that most super-rich people donate money to certain causes (orphanage homes, old age homes, or sponsoring the education of a poor child). This act also brings a thought of harmony in your mind and gives a signal to your subconscious that I am living the life of abundance. The act of donating instills a profound sense of purpose in one's life, affirming one's inherent value and significance (or worth living).

On a spiritual plane, the universe specifically identifies and selects the individual who actively donates money, subsequently directing financial resources towards her as a reward for her generosity (it's like God making his work of giving through her).

You will be surprised to know that the person who donates gets back 10 times the amount she gave. This is the reason why super-rich people donate money to various causes. Be wise and use this secret of the universe to get rich.

If you follow above practice, then following affirmation may help you to shift the reality further.

1. I'm so happy and grateful now that money comes to me in increasing quantities through multiple sources on a continuous basis"- ***Bob Proctor***
2. I deserve to be rich because I add value to other people's lives"-***Unknown***

Let's discuss family aspects of life in the next chapter.

Action Points:

1) Which aspects are missing in your money (Tick):

1. Spiritual
2. Emotional
3. Purpose
4. Money affirmations
5. All the four

2) Read the book Psychology of Money by Morgan Housel.

10

Secret 6: How to Move to the Ladder of Belongingness

****

"If you plan on being anything less than you are capable of being, you will probably be unhappy all the days of your life."
- Abraham Maslow

Before we deep dive into the family aspects of life, let's examine the five levels of living of Abraham Maslow.

According to Abraham Maslow, humans encounter the following five levels of living:

1. Survival and Safety- Look for basic needs
2. Security- Create a guaranteed income source for living

3. Belongingness- Command respect with good behaviour in both family and social circles
4. Self-esteem- Love yourself and live consistently with the highest values
5. Self-actualization- For example writes books or creates works of art or any creative work. It's also called the creator level

It is sad that only 2% of the population reaches the level of self-actualization.

If you examine it, you'll find that we humans grow to the 5th level gradually and exactly at the middle of these levels we encounter belongingness where we command respect with good behaviour in our family and social circles.

This indicates that an individual must address and overcome challenges related to survival, safety, and security as a foundational step. Successfully navigating these issues enables progression up the hierarchy toward belongingness. Achieving this level enhances one's social interactions and deepens connections with others in their community.

In today's time, we inherit both survival and safety from our parents. But we struggle at the security level (where we need to ensure that we have a reliable source of income for living) most of our life because we tie our days of life for time-bound money and that limits our income sources. Let's learn how to be free from time bound money below.

There is an abundance of money, but not of time:

You receive financial compensation in return for dedicating your time, effectively exchanging hours of your life for monetary gain. But, the true worth of this time is much more than the money earned. It is a universally acknowledged truth that while money exists in ample quantities, time does not, rendering it a far more precious commodity. Despite this, the prevalent belief among the vast majority contradicts this reality, valuing money over time. To understand this paradox, we must delve deeper into the origins of such a mindset.

Our educational institutions systematically exclude financial literacy from our curriculum. It appears students are encouraged to remain ignorant about monetary matters. The academic approach focuses on rote memorization of information, encouraging students to simply repeat answers during examinations to progress from one grade to the next. The goal seems to be to guide students through school, give them diplomas or degrees, and integrate them into the workforce.

It's a well-planned system orchestrated by big business houses and executed (or infused) by politicians, bureaucrats (policy-makers), and the education system. They want a large population to work for them. They never teach you about money and that affects your path of the creator level.

*"The poor and middle-class work for money. The rich have money work for them."- **Robert Kiyosaki***

On top of that, the money you earn reduces its value. Look at your 100 dollars which is now equivalent to 30 just in a decade. That means the valuation of your money is reduced by 70%, and so are your savings. You'll feel scammed if you figure out the money. To escape it, learn about money, free yourself from it, and ascend to the creator level.

How to free yourself from time-bound money?

Let's say I have published this book and put around 1000 hours to complete it. I lock my time in this book one time. I can now sell multiple copies of this book for years. This is one way to free myself from time-bound money. You need to explore opportunities that will provide you financial freedom and eliminate the constraints of time-bound earnings.

Free From Time-Bound Money

Figure 4: How to Cultivate Your Inner Voice

Let's learn how to build lasting relationships in the next chapter.

Action Points:

1) Create a list of areas where you can free yourself from time-bound money.

2) Where you find yourself if you measure all the five levels of Abraham Maslow. Write it down below.

11

Secret 7: The Keys to Building a Lasting Relationship (Social)

****

"Trust is the glue of life. It is the most essential ingredient in effective communication. It's the foundational principle that holds all relationships."

- Stephen R. Covey

In this chapter, we will delve into the intricate dynamics of human relationships. Our expectations, which vary from one individual to another, are foundational to these relationships. When someone aligns with the specific criteria we anticipate in a relationship (expectations), a sense of connection is established. This principle holds true across all forms of human connections. Some of them are listed below:

1. The employer has expectations from employees.
2. The wife has certain expectations from her husband or vice versa.
3. My client has expectations for the work they assign to me.
4. My reader has a set of expectations from my book or social media content.
5. I have a set of expectations for my work.
6. You have a certain set of expectations from your client or employer or co-worker.

We always expect something from others in all the above or any other relationship. It is not only restricted to the people around you but also to yourself. For example, I expect great success in all seven spokes of my life (Career, Financial, Spiritual, Physical, Intellectual, Family, and Social). I disconnect from myself if I fail in any of these areas.

'Expectations' are key in any relationship. Relationships flourish if one understands it. For example, you understand your spouse when you spend time with them and know what they expect from you. You gain an extra edge by making this connection.

In the next few chapters, we will look at some tools and techniques to improve your self-awareness and understanding of life.

Action Points:

List down the various people in your life and write down what they expect from you. The below exercise will help you to build better connections once you know their expectations.

Person #1:
Expectations:

Person #2
Expectations:

Person #3
Expectations:

Person #4
Expectations:

Person #5:
Expectations:

Person #6:

Expectations:

Person #7:
Expectations:

Person #8:
Expectations:

12

The Power of
Journaling

"I can recapture everything when I write, my thoughts, my ideals, and my fantasies."

- Anne Frank

The idea of writing this book came to me when I started to document my thoughts in the form of journaling. You express your thoughts in the form of words and archive it for future reference and the same can be converted in the form of a book.

How you build your thought process:

Let's say you attended one of the workshops recently. You

learned a lot of new stuff there. You can weave your life experiences into this new learning and build new thoughts. These thoughts are fleeting, and you lose it if you fail to record it somewhere. Thus, the act of journaling saves your thought process. Some of us also have a habit of sharing their thoughts on social media and they record their life learning in the form of content on such platforms.

Build and maintain the habit of expressing your new learning on platforms like social media, digital device, notebook, notepad or book. It's an act that builds your ability to influence others and make a positive impact in their life by sharing your insights and ideas. It also creates your image of a thought leader.

It has long been revered as a powerful tool for self-exploration and personal growth. By putting pen to paper, we engage in a private dialogue with our innermost thoughts, emotions, and experiences, creating a sacred space for self-reflection and introspection. However, journaling is more than mere documentation of events; it is a conduit for delving into the depths of our psyche, uncovering hidden truths, and unlocking our true potential. Let's understand the few benefits of journaling below.

Journaling as a Mirror to the Soul

At its core, journaling serves as a mirror that reflects our inner world. Through the process of committing our thoughts and feelings to paper, we gain clarity and insights that might otherwise remain obscured by the noise of daily life. Like a skilled therapist, the journal becomes a confidant, a non-judgmental space where we can freely explore our deepest desires, fears, and vulnerabilities without the constraints of external pressures or societal norms.

The Therapeutic Benefits of Journaling

Numerous studies have highlighted the therapeutic benefits of journaling, solidifying its place as a powerful tool for self-discovery and emotional healing. In a landmark study by Dr. James W. Pennebaker, participants who wrote about traumatic experiences, experienced a significant improvement in physical and mental health compared to those who did not. The act of expressing emotions through writing has been shown to reduce stress, alleviate symptoms of depression and anxiety, and even boost immune function.

Ultimately, the practice of journaling holds the potential to cultivate a more compassionate, self-aware, and resilient society. By encouraging introspection, emotional intelligence, and empathy, journaling can bridge divides, foster understanding, and inspire positive change on both individual and collective levels.

13

How to Cultivate our Inner Voice

****

"Don't let the noise of others' opinions drown out your own inner voice."

- Steve Jobs

The consequences of neglecting our intuitive voice echo across all facets of our existence, casting long shadows upon our personal and professional lives. We may find ourselves mired in unfulfilling relationships, trapped in careers that stifle our passions, or plagued by a persistent sense of empti-ness and disconnection, unable to discern the path that truly resonates with our souls.

This disconnect from our intuitive nature carries grave implications, for it is this very connection that serves as our compass, guiding us through life's complexities with clarity and authenticity. Without it, we risk losing touch with our deepest truths, succumbing to a life of reactivity, where we merely respond to external stimuli rather than aligning our actions with our innermost desires and highest potentials.

Moreover, our decision-making process becomes stunted, relying solely on logic and external influences, rather than tapping into the rich tapestry of our inner wisdom, woven from the threads of our experiences, emotions, and deep self-knowledge.

Thus, understanding certain key terms is essential to harness our inner voice. These concepts serve as guideposts, illuminating the path toward self-discovery and informed decision-making.

Let us unravel the layers of meaning concealed within these words, for they hold the power to catalyze a heightened state of awareness and alignment with our innermost selves.

Intuition: Often described as a 'gut feeling' or an inexplicable hunch, intuition is a whisper from the depths of our subconscious, signaling us to heed its call. It is the culmination of our experiences, knowledge, and emotional intelligence, distilled into a silent, yet profound, voice that guides our actions. Like a compass in the midst of life's storms, intuition offers us a sense of direction when reason alone falls short.

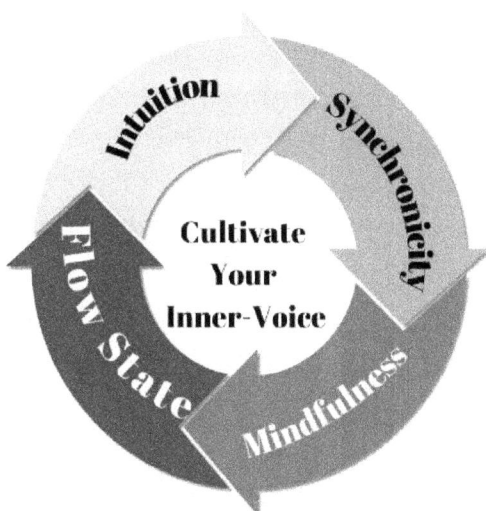

Figure 5: How to Cultivate Your Inner Voice

Synchronicity: Synchronicity refers to the mystical convergence of seemingly unrelated events, ideas, or experiences in a profoundly meaningful way. These moments of chance, where the universe appears to conspire in our favor, can serve as potent affirmations of our intuitive learnings, and that open the path of our chosen destination.

Mindfulness: Like a calming balm, mindfulness cultivates the stillness necessary to tune into the subtle whispers of our intuition. By anchoring our awareness in the present moment, we create a sacred space where our inner voice can resonate with clarity, unburdened by the incessant chatter of the mind or the distractions of the external world.

Flow State: Have you ever experienced those moments of effortless concentration, where time seems to dissolve, and your actions align seamlessly with your goals? This is the flow state, a heightened state of consciousness where our intuition and skills coalesce, propelling us toward peak performance and profound fulfillment.

As we go deeper into all the above terms, we uncover our inner voice. It helps us to move towards a clearer path of our life.

14

Meditation: The Inner Dialogue

****

"As I walk I meditate on the word of God. It comforts me."
- Lailah Gifty Akita

By following this guided meditation, you will learn to quiet the incessant chatter of the external world and engage in a reflective dialogue with your inner self. This practice will allow you to peel away the layers of distraction and noise, revealing the core of your being and the immense wisdom it holds.

Materials or prerequisites: A quiet, undisturbed space and a comfortable seated position. An open mind and a willingness to embrace the journey inward.

Steps:

I. Preparing for the Journey

Find a quiet, comfortable space where you can sit undisturbed.

Settle into a seated position that allows your spine to remain upright yet relaxed.

Take a few deep breaths, inhaling slowly through your nose and exhaling gently through your mouth.

With each exhalation, release any lingering thoughts or tensions, creating a blank canvas for your inner exploration.

II. Focused Breathing: The Gateway Within

Bring your attention to your natural rhythm of breathing.

Inhale slowly, allowing your belly to expand, and exhale fully, letting your abdomen gently contract.

As you breathe, envision each inhalation as a cleansing stream of energy, washing away the distractions of the external world.

With each exhalation, feel yourself sinking deeper into a state of calmness and presence.

Continue this rhythmic breathing for several minutes, until you feel a sense of grounded tranquility enveloping your being.

III. Visualization: The Journey Within

With your mind settled and your body relaxed, begin to

visualize a serene, natural environment that resonates with your inner peace.

It could be a secluded beach, a lush forest, or a mountain-top overlooking a panoramic vista.

Immerse yourself in the sights, sounds, and sensations of this place, allowing it to become a vibrant rainbow of your imagination.

As you explore this inner landscape, you may notice a path emerging before you, inviting you to venture deeper within.

Follow this path, trusting that it will lead you to the heart of your inner sanctum, where the whispers of your intuition reside.

IV. The Inner Dialogue: Posing Questions, Receiving Insights

Upon reaching the innermost chamber of your being, take a moment to settle into the stillness that permeates this sacred space.

Formulate a question, a burning inquiry that you have long sought to answer, and pose it to the silence that surrounds you.

Do not force an immediate response; instead, cultivate a state of receptive listening, allowing the answer to emerge from the depths of your intuitive wisdom.

The reply may come as a gentle whisper, a vivid image, or a profound feeling that resonates within your core.

Embrace this insight, letting it permeate your being, and explore any additional questions that arise from this new-found understanding.

V. Returning to the Outer World

When you feel complete with your inner dialogue, take a few deep breaths and begin to shift your awareness back to your physical surroundings.

Gently wiggle your fingers and toes, reawakening your connection to your body.

With a renewed sense of clarity and inner knowing, open your eyes and take in the world around you with fresh perspectives.

Carry the insights and wisdom gained from your inner journey with you, allowing them to guide your actions and inform your decisions throughout your day.

Tips and Warnings:

Approach this practice with patience and an open mind. The ability to connect with your inner voice may take time and consistent effort to develop.

If your mind wanders, gently guide it back to your breath or visualization without judgment. Distractions are natural; the key is to remain focused on your intention.

Avoid forcing insights or answers; trust that they will emerge when the time is right, and let the process unfold organically.

Be mindful of the emotional or psychological content that may arise during your inner dialogue. If it becomes overwhelming, gently shift your focus or consider seeking professional support.

15

The Art of Mindful Listening

****

"You cannot truly listen to anyone and do anything else at the same time."

- M. Scott Peck

By cultivating the art of mindful listening, you will unlock a gateway to deeper understanding, both within yourself and in your connections with others. This practice transcends mere hearing to embrace a state of full presence and receptivity, allowing you to grasp the nuances of communication that often go unnoticed. Through mindful listening, you will develop the capacity to truly comprehend the spoken and unspoken layers of interaction, fostering meaningful relationships and heightening your self-awareness. *Nirupan* (discourse) and *Shravan* (listening) of the scripture *Shrimat Dasbodh*, preaches this aspect of life to the truest and fullest sense.

Materials or Prerequisites: An open mind and a willingness to be present. A quiet environment, free from distractions, where you can focus your undivided attention.

How to Practice Active Listening: Practice following steps for active listening.

1. When the other person begins to speak, resist the urge to formulate a response or allow your mind to wander.

2. Focus your entire being on their words, tone, and body language, as if they were the only thing that existed in that moment.

3. Periodically paraphrase or summarize what you have heard, to ensure you are accurately comprehending the message and to demonstrate your engagement.

4. Observe any nonverbal cues, such as facial expressions, gestures, or shifts in energy, as these can convey unspoken emotions or intentions.

5. Resist the temptation to interrupt or interject with your own thoughts or experiences; allow the speaker to fully express themselves before responding.

How to Develop Empathy and Emotional Intelligence through Active Listening: You can develop this ability by applying the following steps.

1. As you listen, endeavor to step into the speaker's

shoes, imagining how they might be feeling or perceiving the situation.

2. Attune yourself to the emotional undercurrents beneath the words, picking up on subtle inflections or energy shifts that reveal deeper layers of meaning.

3. Ask clarifying questions that demonstrate your desire to truly understand, not merely gather information.

4. Offer empathetic acknowledgments or reflections, validating the speaker's experience without judgment or dismissal.

5. Practice self-awareness, noticing any personal biases, assumptions, or emotional triggers that may cloud your ability to listen objectively.

Tips and Warnings:

1. Approach mindful listening with patience and compassion, both for yourself and for others. It is a skill that requires consistent practice and dedication.

2. Avoid multitasking or allowing your mind to wander during conversations; focusing your full attention is essential for true understanding.

3. Suspend judgment and approach each interaction with fresh eyes and an open heart.

4. If you find yourself becoming emotionally triggered or overwhelmed during a conversation, pause and take a few deep breaths to re-center yourself before continuing.

5. Remember that mindful listening is not about agreeing

or validating every perspective; it is about truly comprehending the experiences and viewpoints of others.

16

How to Define Your Financial Vision

"Invest first in education. In reality, the only real asset you have is your mind, the most powerful tool we have dominion over."

- Robert Kiyosaki

As said by Robert Kiyosaki in one of his quotes "Financial freedom is a mental, emotional and educational process." Let's work on this aspect of money in this chapter by using the below steps.

Goal: Craft a comprehensive financial plan that aligns with your deepest aspirations, values, and life goals.

Materials Needed:

1. A journal or notebook
2. A quiet, distraction-free environment
3. An open and reflective mindset

Overview: Creating a financial plan begins with envisioning the life you desire. This step involves exploring your core values, defining your long-term goals, and imagining the future you want to manifest. By establishing a clear vision, you'll have a guiding light to shape your financial decisions and strategies.

Detailed Steps:

1. Reflect on your core values and what truly matters to you. Consider questions like "What brings you joy and fulfillment?" "What kind of impact do you want to make in the world?" "How do you want to be remembered?"
2. Visualize your ideal life 5, 10, 20, or even 30 years from now. Imagine yourself living in alignment with your values and achieving your most cherished goals. What does this future look like? Where do you live? What are you doing? Who surrounds you?
3. Write down this vision in vivid detail, capturing the sights, sounds, emotions, and sensations. Describe your day-to-day life, your relationships, your work or

creative pursuits, and the environments that energize you.

4. Identify the specific goals and milestones that comprise this vision. Break them down into tangible, measurable objectives, such as the total amount needed for financial independence, starting a business, pursuing education, or engaging in philanthropic endeavors.

5. Prioritize these goals based on their importance and the time frames in which you'd like to achieve them.

In the above steps, you have to clearly define your financial freedom amount and work on achieving this milestone first.

Tips and Warnings:

- Be bold in your vision. Don't let fear or self-doubt limit your aspirations.
- Revisit and refine your vision periodically as your circumstances and priorities evolve.
- Avoid setting goals solely based on societal expectations or external pressures.
- Remember that your financial plan is a means to an end, not an end in itself.

Checking for Understanding:

Your vision should be a vivid, emotionally resonant depiction of the life you genuinely want to lead. It should inspire you and serve as a touchstone for the subsequent steps in crafting your financial canvas.

17

Find Your Passion

"Your purpose in life is to find your purpose and give your life whole heart and soul to it."
- Buddha

In this chapter, we'll discover your true passions and learn how to seamlessly integrate them into your life path.

Materials or prerequisites:

- An open and introspective mindset
- A willingness to explore and experiment
- Basic self-reflection tools (e.g., journal, meditation practice)

Overview of the steps:

- Reflect on your deepest interests and the activities that energize you
- Identify the underlying themes and patterns in your passions
- Explore life paths that align with your passions
- Strategically integrate your passions into your work
- Continuously refine and adjust as your passions evolve

Detailed steps:

I. Uncover Your True Passions:

- Engage in self-reflection exercises to identify the activities, subjects, or causes that bring you joy and a sense of purpose.
- Explore your childhood dreams, hobbies, and interests for clues to your innate passions.
- Pay attention to the tasks or projects that leave you feeling energized and fulfilled.
- Note the times when you lose track of time due to deep engagement and enjoyment.

II. Identify Underlying Themes and Patterns:

- Analyze the common threads that run through your various passions and interests.
- Look for broader themes, such as creativity, problem-

solving, helping others, or working with specific groups or subjects.

- Recognize the skills, values, and personality traits that are consistently present in your passionate pursuits.

III. Explore Life Paths Aligned with Your Passions:

- Research on work, industries, and roles that intersect with your identified themes and interests.
- Consider both traditional and unconventional paths, as well as opportunities to create your own niche.
- Assess how this new option could help you grow, make a difference, and feel fulfilled.

IV. Strategically Integrate Your Passions:

- Identify ways to incorporate your passions into your current role or workplace.
- Volunteer, take on side projects, or join committees that allow you to explore your interests.
- Propose ideas or initiatives that align with your passions and benefit your organization.
- Consider entrepreneurial ventures or freelance opportunities that enable you to pursue your passions more directly.

V. Continuously Refine and Adjust:

- Embrace the understanding that your passions may evolve over time.
- Periodically reassess your interests and the alignment between your work and passions.
- Be open to pivots, course corrections, or entirely new paths as your passions shift.
- Continuously seek opportunities to deepen your engagement with the activities and causes you care about most.

Tips and Best Practices:

- Be patient and persistent in your pursuit of passion integration; it may take time and incremental steps.
- Seek out mentors or role models who have successfully aligned their work with their passions.
- Embrace a growth mindset and be willing to learn new skills or acquire knowledge to bridge the gap between your passions and career aspirations.
- Communicate your passions and their value to your employer or potential employers.
- Strike a balance between following your passions and maintaining financial stability and practical considerations.

Potential Pitfalls:

- Becoming overly idealistic or unrealistic in your expectations for seamless passion integration.

- Struggling with decision paralysis due to an over-whelming number of potential paths.
- Neglecting practical considerations, such as financial stability or career progression opportunities.
- Allowing external influences or societal pressures to overshadow your true passions and interests.
- Failing to continuously reevaluate and adjust your path as your passions evolve.

Troubleshooting and Solutions:

- If you struggle to identify your true passions, seek guidance from a career coach or mentor, or explore self-discovery workshops or exercises.
- If your current role or workplace does not allow for passion integration, consider a strategic job change, entrepreneurial ventures, or pursuing your passions through side projects or volunteering.
- If you face resistance or lack of support from your em-ployer, try to clearly articulate the value and benefits of passion integration, or explore alternative paths.
- If your passions change or evolve, embrace the oppor-tunity for growth and adjustment.

In the next few chapters, we'll dive deeper and uncover your true insights (core). It contains questionnaires, a plan-ner, a daily action list, and affirmations.

18

Define Your Dream Life

"Good teaching is more a giving of right questions than a giving of right answers."

- Joseph Albers

Before looking for answers, it's important to carefully create your questions. The better and more specific your questions are, the better the answers you'll get. Write down the answer to the following questions. It will help you to decode your dream life.

A. What are my big dreams in life?

B. What is that first step I can take to reach my dreams?

C. What plan do I need to make today to reach that dream?

D. What are two things I must do today to reach those dreams - no matter what?

E. What things do I have that will help me achieve my dreams?

19

Personal Monthly Planner

****

"The people who get things done, who lead, who grow, and who make an impact...those people have goals."

- Seth Goddin

It's my personal monthly planner. Every month I write one major goal of my life in this column and accomplish it. It helps me to reach that big dream step by step. Writing and seeing goals help us to accomplish it fast and that's the reason I have given space in each of the columns for this exercise below. You can write down your monthly goal in your diary or calendar.

My Monthly Goals Planner:

Months	Goals
January	
February	
March	
April	
May	
June	
July	
August	
September	
October	
November	
December	

Your monthly planner acts like a map. It shows you destination in the form of a goal. Additionally, you can create bi-monthly, quarterly, and half-yearly goal lists. Also, you can set one goal in a year and take bolder action to accomplish it.

20

My Daily Action List

"There is only one success- to be able to spend your life in your own way."

- Christopher Morley

Apart from a monthly planner, you need to create your daily action list. You accomplish most of your goals by taking daily action or let's say your life changes the moment you start taking action. What five actions do I need to take today to accomplish my short-term or long-term goals? You can list it in the following manner.

Action #1- Read the 10 pages of the book of my subject of interest.

Action #2- Write/review 300 words of my book project

Action #3- Watch one video related to my subject learning

Action #4- Create engaging content for social media platforms and expand the network by establishing more connections.

Action #5- Review one goal and measure it in terms of both progress and time. For example, the total number of pages finished in my book and the time required to add a new chapter in it.

You must commit yourself to accomplishing everything from your daily to-do list. Imagine your life one year from now. All the small actions taken today will yield great results after one year. You can see the impact of these changes in your life.

*"Inaction breeds doubt and fear. Action breeds confidence and courage. If you want to conquer fear, do not sit home and think about it. Go out and get busy". -**Dale Carnegie***

Write your daily action list below.

Action #1-

Action #2-

Action #3-

Action #4-

Action #5-

Action #6-

Action #7-

Action #8-

21

Affirmations

"When a thought of anger, jealousy, fear or worry creeps in just say the affirmation. The way to fight darkness is with light –the way to fight cold is with heat -the way to overcome evils is with good. Affirm the good, and the bad will vanish"
- Frederick Elias Andrews

A tiny seed has the potential to grow into a giant tree. It just needs light, soil, water, and fertilizer in the right amount. All the ingredients are essential for its growth. Each part of this book is strategically divided into these parts: 1) Transformation secrets (light), 2) Tools and techniques (soil), and 3) Questionnaire and planner to define your life (water). In this chapter, we introduced affirmations that will help you to use it like fertilizers. We have divided affirmation mainly into the following parts:

1. Physical Health Affirmations
2. Emotional Health Affirmations
3. Spiritual Health Affirmations
4. Mental Health Affirmations

Choose a few from each category and say them in your mind in the morning, afternoon, and evening time. It will boost your growth further.

Physical Health Affirmations

1. Every day my health is getting better and better
2. I love to take care of my body and respect its needs
3. I deserve healthy and a happy life
4. I feed my body with nutritious foods that increase vitality
5. With each heartbeat, I committed to my great health
6. With every breath, I multiply my healing power
7. With every step, I'm getting better, better and better
8. I feed my body with healthy and nutritious food and that increases its vitality

Emotional Health Affirmations

1. My emotions create my life and I shape it with my will
2. I accept the emotions that serve my purpose and growth
3. With every breath, I create positive emotions
4. It is my right to be at peace and to be healed emotionally

Spiritual Health Affirmations

1. My soul is lifted with every breath I take
2. I nourish my soul with meditation
3. My soul is eternal and helping me to sail the life journey smoothly
4. I am a divine creator and manifest my dreams
5. My current life path is decided by God and I believe and accept it

Mental Health Affirmations

1. I am devoted to my mental health and I hold it in high regard
2. There is peace in the way I communicate and act
3. My thoughts, words, and actions bring in me complete tranquility
4. With each passing day, I find greater inner calmness and mental strength
5. I deserve mental clarity, love, and joy
6. I am committed to the well-being of my mental health and I embrace it with love, joy, and bliss
7. I am mindful of my mental and physical well-being

22

Conclusion

"It is not the strongest of the species that survives, nor the most intelligent, but the most responsive to change."
- Charles Darwin

We humans survive because we respond to the changes and adapt to the new possibilities. We have the capability to rediscover ourselves so many times. Life is like sensing the danger before we face it and preparing ourselves to overcome it (do or die).

The things we do today decide our future. Most of us know that to get the result Y, we need to do X (preparing for tomorrow or defining the future outcome). It's like I am going to make my body more flexible (Y) if I do Yoga (X). But most of us fail to detect the changes and burden ourselves with so many things and lose touch with our inner voice (inner self) and fail to define any outcome like the above. If we play it on health aspects, then one day life will whisper "You are losing your health and need to take charge of it" and if you ignore this whisper (warning) and grind yourselves further, then it will surely lead to a decline in physical health. You just need to give time to heal it at both physical and mental levels. Take a break and refill it before you move further. Our body is so flexible that it becomes coherent to the new changes and heals years of damage fast as it is designed that way only (it wants to survive). Here, you just need to pay attention to the health aspect of your life and it will take care of it.

This principle applies uniformly across all the remaining six facets of life mentioned in this book. Consider, for instance, the spiritual aspects. By focusing on your spirituality, you establish a deeper connection with your higher self.

Same way, new knowledge can be acquired through books, training, or any other source if you need new learning in life. You just have to be a great learner.

If you want to leave your outdated career, then create the space for a new one and work around it.

If there is a gap between expenses and income and if you find that expenses are higher than the earned income, then you need to fill this gap by creating more income sources (or multiple income sources) to overcome these challenges.

Your family plays a crucial role in your success. You need support from your spouse or other family members to make any important decision in life. Present yourself as a capable person who not only takes calculated risks but also has the power to overcome any crises. You can start working on this change by making small decisions.

Your social status is closely tied to your lifestyle, and that finds ground in the seven pivotal secrets of transformation outlined in this book. This concept echoes a sentiment by T Harv Eker, "What you do here you do everywhere," highlighting the interconnectivity between personal actions and social perception. The facets of your life, including your health, financial status, emotional well-being, intellectual depth, and the strength of your relationships within both social and familial networks, are closely observed by those around you. These aspects collectively influence how you project yourself in every environment, thereby shaping the quality of your interactions and the nature of your relationships with others.

It is clear from above that you need awareness to overcome the challenges of all the seven spokes of life. It's a roadmap of your life that helps you to show the life path.

I began writing this book with my personal story and discussed the seven spokes of life one by one. Subsequently, I transitioned to discussing the tools and techniques segment, where I imparted a detailed insight that I personally utilize. The purpose of this book is to add value in your life. I have read many books and learned something valuable from each of them. I have briefly summarized this book in the following words.

"In order to fly a plane in the sky, a pilot needs to undergo training. He/she needs to understand the functions of all the buttons of the cockpit. All the seven-spoke of life act like a button of your life plane. You can fly it if you know the functions of them (buttons)".

In this book, I have endeavored to enlighten you on

the existence and functionality of various metaphorical "life buttons." These buttons, I explain, are integral components of your life's dashboard, and understanding their functions is crucial for navigating the journey of your existence. By mastering the operations of each, you are empowered to pilot the aircraft of your life with confidence and skill through the vast skies of possibility.

Feel free to give me feedback on this book, on my email ID swapsab@gmail.com. I will love to hear from you and appreciate your review.

23

Find Me Here

LinkedIn

https://www.linkedin.com/in/swapnilbharate/

Instagram

https://www.instagram.com/swapsab/

Facebook

https://www.facebook.com/swapnil.bharate.3

COMPANY- SP AND SS LTD

https://spandssltd.co.uk

24

Bibliography

Allen, David (2001). Getting Things Done: The Art of Stress-Free Productivity. London, UK: Piatkus.

Kiyosaki, Robert (1999). Rich Dad's Cashflow Quadrant: Guide to Financial Freedom. New York, USA: Warner Books.

Goleman, Daniel (2021). Emotional Intelligence. New Delhi, Bloomsbury India.

Dispenza, Joe (2017). Becoming Supernatural: How Common People Are Doing the Uncommon. New Delhi: Penguin Random House India.

Tracy, Brian (2011). No Excuses!: The Power of Self-Discipline for Success in Your Life. India, Khushi Book.

Harari, Yuval Noah (2017). Homo Deus: A Brief History of Tomorrow. London, UK: Penguin Random House.

Dweck, Carol (2006). Mindset: The New Psychology of Success. New York, USA: Robinson.

Canfield, Jack (2011). The Power of Focus: How to Hit Your Business, Personal and Financial Targets with Confidence and Certainty. USA: Vermillion.

Koch, Richard (2008). The 80/20 Principle: The Secret to Achieving More with Less. New York, USA: Crown Business.

DeMarco, MJ (2017). Unscripted: Life, Liberty, and the Pursuit of Entrepreneurship. USA: Viperion Corporation.

DeMarco, MJ (2017). The Millionaire Fastlane: Crack The Code To Wealth And Live Rich For A Lifetime. Noida, India: Manjul Publishing House Pvt Ltd.

Cardone, Grant (2011). The 10X Rule: The Only Difference Between Success. USA: Wiley.

25

Recommended Reading
for You

Title	Author
Ageless Body Timeless Mind	Deepak Chopra
Alchemist	Paulo Coelho
Atomic Habits	James Clear
Black Box Thinking	Matthew Syed
CEO Excellence: Six Mindsets that Distinguish the Best Leaders from the rest	Carolyn Dewar, Scott Keller, Vikram Malhotra
I am Malala	Malala Yousafzai
Management and Organizational Behaviour	Laurie Mullins

Manual of the Warrior of Light	Paulo Coelho
Maximizing Your Memory	Jonathan Hancock
Peace of Mind	Thich Nhat Hanh
Stress: The Psychology of Managing Pressure	DK
The 21 Irrefutable Laws of Leadership	John Maxwell
The 7 Habits of Highly Effective People	Stephen R Covey
The Diary of a CEO	Steven Bartlett
The Everyday Hero Manifesto	Robin Sharma
The Infinite Game	Simon Sinek
The Psychology of Money	Morgan Housel
The Shredded Chef: 125 Recipes for Building Muscle	Michael Matthews
Why Has Nobody Told Me This Before?	Julie Smith
Wings of Fire	A P J Abdul Kalam

Notes:

Notes:

www.ingramcontent.com/pod-product-compliance
Lightning Source LLC
Chambersburg PA
CBHW071241020426
42333CB00015B/1567